Phyllis

Happy 41st

1979

Love

Judy —

# COMPULSIVE COOKERY

# COMPULSIVE COOKERY

## A Guide to the Fine Art of Neurotic Gastronomy

### Dr. Maureen Bendick, Ph.D.

McClelland and Stewart Limited

McClelland and Stewart Limited
*The Canadian Publishers*
25 Hollinger Road, Toronto

0-7710-1191-1

# Contents

Introduction/7
**Aboulia**
Sole with Shrimp
(Abouliabaisse)/9
**Acrophobia**
Low Lemon Chicken/10
**Agoraphobia**
Tamales Together/13
**Alcoholism**
Secret-Drinker Soup/14
Bourbon Eggs/14
**Amnesia**
Unforgettable Veal/17
**Anal Personality**
Oxtail Ragoût/18
**Anxiety**
Pork Chops Piquant/20
**Blocking**
Sole Fouquet/23
**Bruxism**
Stuffed Spareribs/24
**Castration Anxiety**
Stuffed Zucchini with
Father's Frankfurters/27

**Catalepsy and Stereotypy**
Boring Bearnaise/28
**Catatonia**
Clam Chowder/31
**Claustrophobia**
Chili Con Queso/32
**Compulsive Overeating**
Overstuffed Mushrooms/33
**Cyclothymic Personality**
Paella/34
**Electra or Oedipus Complex**
Mom's Lemon Pie/38
**Euphoria**
Sangria Elan/38
**Exhibitionism**
Rump Round/41
Orange Potato Balls/41

**Fetishism**
Bosom de Poulet/42
**Flagellant**
Baked Flank Steak Flagellata/45
**Frigidity**
Cold Brocolli Rémoulade/46
**Gilles de la Tourette Syndrome**
Four-Letter Veal (or pork)/49
**Grandiosity**
Crown Ribs of Lamb/50
Celeriac/51
**Group Therapy**
Fondue – with Hot Mustard,
Bearnaise, and Curry Sauces/52/53
**Hypochondriasis**
Casserole Santé/55
**Hysteria**
Strawberry Glee/56
**Impotence**
Impotence Soufflé/57
**Inhibition**
Pardon-me-Pork/58
**Kleptomania**
Tournedos Rossini/61
Potato and Dill Soup/61

**Masochism**
Sufferers' Roast Wellington/62
**Melancholia**
Blue Cabbage/63
**Multiple Personality**
Sauerbraten mit
Yorkshire Pudding/65
**Narcolepsy**
Cabbage Rolls and Rest/67
**Nymphomania**
Chicken Chow Mein
(Won Ton Hussy)/69
Egg Foo Jung/69
**Obsessive Compulsive Personality**
Perfectly Square Ravioli/70
**Paranoia**
Paranoid Hot Pot – with Dill
and Horseradish Sauces/73
**Perseveration**
Enchilladas Encore/74
**Polymorphous Perverse**
Strawberries Jubilee/76
Chocolate Pie/77
Banana Trifle/77
Coffee Bavarian Cream/77

**Psychoanalysis**
Stuffed Artichokes/79
**Pyromania**
Bananas Flambé/80
**Rorschach Inkblot Test**
Ham and Beef Rouladen/83
**Sadism**
Chicken à la Sade/84
Chicken Meany/85
**Sibling Rivalry**
Crêpes Nicole/86
**Satyriasis or Don Juanism**
Shashlik/89
**Somnambulism**
Coffee Liqueur/90
**Tension Headache**
Steak Tartare/91
**Voyeurism**
Undressed Breast of Chicken/92
**Xenophobia**
Chiou Tzu/95
**Zeitgarnik Effect**
Complete German Potato Salad/96

**For Floyd in spite of everything**

**Acknowledgement**

Although this book bears only one author's name, it was actually written in collaboration with a friend and professional colleague, Sharon McCollough.

While she does not cook, she made valuable contributions to the psychological texts and in co-writing helped make this book a playful and enjoyable endeavour. We both hope that readers will have as much fun with it as we had in creating it.

## Introduction

This is a cookbook for everybody. After many years of clinical practice, I have realized that we all have quirks that are wonderfully varied and that if we got rid of them, the world would be a dull and predictable place. There is no such entity as the "normal" person, there are only variations on peculiarity. Some of these peccadilloes have been duly catalogued by the scientists and psychotherapists and it is these familiar and well-respected symptoms that are presented in this book. There are a few esoteric syndromes, such as aboulia and catalepsy, but many of you will be familiar, in some fashion, with the problems engendered by claustrophobia or amnesia.

It is my opinion that quirks are to be lived with, enjoyed, understood, and respected, so I am offering a cookbook in which there are recipes for many symptoms which are classified as "neurotic" (or worse). Learn to live with your kinks and cook with your quirks. Herein, then, a cookbook for the neurotic, with recipes to match your symptoms and some symptoms you may not yet have tried.

# Aboulia

Aboulia is a psychological condition marked by the inability to make even simple decisions. The most helpful approach for you would seem to be in offering you only *one* recipe – and no options on ingredients. If you suffer from aboulia, the following whole menu is provided so that you won't have to falter over what to serve with what.

If you can't decide whether or not you have aboulia – you probably do.

## Sole with Shrimp (Abouliabaisse)

8 fillets of sole, small or medium
2 tbsp. margarine or butter
1 cup cooked shrimp
1 cup mushrooms
small carton sour cream
½ small package of process cheese
salt and pepper
ground dill weed

Fry or broil the sole quickly in butter or margarine (about 3 minutes per side). Set aside in warm oven while making sauce. Place the sour cream and the process cheese in double boiler and heat until these melt into a creamy sauce. Sauté the cooked shrimp and mushrooms in butter or margarine until the mushrooms are barely cooked. To serve this dish at its best, warm a platter and place the sole on it, then pour over the cream sauce, sprinkle the top with the mushrooms and shrimp and add a dash of dill just before serving.

Serve this with carrots cooked quickly, then steeped in butter with a jot of cayenne pepper, and arrange the carrots around the platter of sole.

For a nice addition, scoop out tiny potato balls with a melon scoop and cook them in butter with ½ cup white wine or sherry. Sprinkle the potatoes with parsley and serve.

Serves 4.

# Acrophobia

Acrophobia is a morbid fear of heights often found in people who have no other neurotic symptoms. The ideal menu for the acrophobic would be pancakes cooked over a low hibachi while lying on your stomach. If these location suggestions aren't feasible, try the following marvellous recipe for Low Lemon Chicken, and sit down while cooking it.

## Low Lemon Chicken

2 cut-up fryers (1 lb. per person)
½ cup cream
1 lemon
½ cup white wine
1 tbsp. grated lemon peel
1 tbsp. grated orange peel
salt and pepper
butter
2 tbsp. grated parmesan cheese (opt.)

Brown the chicken in hot, foaming butter until it is partially cooked. Add the wine while the pan is still hot and then reduce the heat. Add the cream, the salt and pepper, and 1 tbsp. each of the grated lemon and orange peel. (These come in prepared form now and are excellent.) Then slice the fresh lemon over the chicken – or half of it if you like a little less lemony taste. Cook for about 20 minutes or until done to your taste. It adds a nice zest to sprinkle the chicken with parmesan cheese and run it under the broiler just before serving.

A nice side dish with the excellent chicken is celery root, sliced, cooked and dotted with butter and parsley.

Serves 4.

# Agoraphobia

Agoraphobia is an irrational fear of wide, open places and spaces. The agoraphobic is, in contrast to the claustrophobic, quite content in closets, coalbins, and crowded elevators, but he becomes very anxious in parts of Saskatchewan.

The agoraphobic should first rent an apartment with a very small kitchen and then put in lots of extra cupboards and pull the blinds. Instead of a vast expanse of green salad or a sea of soup – cook up a dinner contained in one pot (with a lid) and ask six people over to eat with you . . . in the kitchen.

An excellent dish for the agoraphobic is tamale pie.

## Tamales Together

½ lb. pork sausage
1 lb. ground beef
1 clove garlic
1 cup diced celery
2 cups whole corn
1 cup pitted ripe olives
1 cup chopped onions
1 large can tomatoes
1½ cups grated cheddar cheese
½ cup cornmeal
1 tsp. salt
3 tsp. chili powder
1 tsp. dry mustard

Sauté the sausage, beef and onions and brown them slightly. Add the celery and garlic and sauté 5 minutes. Then add the tomatoes, corn, salt, and chili powder and simmer for about 15 minutes. Stir in the cornmeal slowly and cook until the mixture is thick. Add the olives. Put it in a greased 2-quart casserole and top with grated cheese. Bake at 350° for about 45 minutes.

Serve with tossed green salad using two or three kinds of lettuce and your favourite vegetables. With French bread, doused with garlic butter, it's a complete meal.

Serves 4.

# Alcoholism

Cooking is a convenient cover for the person suffering from addiction to alcohol. While it is true that drinking and driving don't mix, you've never heard anyone saying "don't sip and sauté" or "if you belt, don't baste." Certainly the French have established that the only successful alcoholic is the subtle alcoholic. Should you suffer from this syndrome, secrete your supply of "sauce" in the kitchen and combine your cultivation of cirrhosis with the consumption of "cuisine continentale." If you are truly an alcoholic, the following recipes won't ˙ help you get over the problem, but they will make it easier for you to get away with it.

## Secret-Drinker Soup

1 can consommé soup
1 stick of cinnamon
1 cup dry red wine
2 whole cloves

Quietly sneak out to the kitchen 20 minutes before dinner, empty a can of consommé into a saucepan, measure off a can of red wine, and add it to the bouillon. (You may then take this opportunity to turn your back on the living room, pour another canful of red wine, and drink it.) Bring the soup to a boil then reduce the heat to simmer and add cinnamon and cloves. Let it simmer for about 15 minutes and remove the cloves and cinnamon sticks before serving. It's really quite a good soup and if anyone asks what makes for the zingy flavour, you can always claim it's the cloves.

Serves 4.

## Bourbon Eggs

For the real student of serious subtle drinking here is an early morning eye-opener. For those of you who have not yet taken to drinking in the morning, you might want to try it just because it tastes so good. Don't let the sound of the A.M. booze discourage you – it really is a delicious breakfast dish served with a rasher of bacon and toasted English muffins.

6 eggs
1 3 oz. package of cream cheese
chopped mushrooms or chives
butter or margarine
salt and pepper
½ jigger bourbon or rum

Lightly beat the eggs* in a mixing bowl, add salt and pepper, chives, and the cream cheese chopped into cubes. Blend in the rum or bourbon, stir it all and pour into a medium hot frying pan coated with foaming butter. Cook as you would ordinary scrambled eggs. The cheese will remain slightly lumpy when the eggs are done, so don't overdo the eggs to get the lumps out.

*see section on Sadism

# Amnesia

Amnesia is a sudden and profound loss of memory for recent and past events. This condition should be distinguished from similar but temporary states such as are encountered after parties and before public-speaking engagements. The wonderful thing about amnesia as a way of life is that no one can blame you when they find all those unmailed letters over the visor in the car.

To simplify matters for the amnesiac, we will give you one short recipe with very little to remember, but we also suggest you take the book with you to the store when shopping for the ingredients – just in case. And when you get all those compliments after dinner, accept them graciously – you *did* cook it, you know.

### Unforgettable Veal

8 veal patties or slices
2 eggs
1 cup dry bread crumbs
2 tbsp. margarine or oil
garlic powder, 2 cloves, chopped
1 large can tomato sauce
salt and pepper
¼ tsp. basil
8 oz. mozzarella cheese

Pound the veal lightly if it is in slices. Season with salt and pepper and dip in the lightly beaten eggs and then in the bread crumbs. Heat the oil or margarine in a hot frying pan and quickly brown the veal on both sides. Remove it to a shallow baking dish. If there is excess oil, pour it out and add to the pan the tomato sauce, garlic, basil, and a little pepper. Simmer this for a few minutes, then pour it over the veal and top it with the mozzarella. Bake in a 350° oven for about 30 minutes.

This is nice served with fresh broccoli and sliced sweet onions seasoned with a tiny bit of oregano.

Serves 4.

# Anal Personality

Anal characteristics were first identified by Freud. These traits are present in people who had a ghastly experience during their toilet training and who have later grown into super-clean stubbornly rigid, withholding adults. Anal personalities try to repress the unpleasant past and forget all those nasty battles over control. As adults, they are generally closed off people who like to store up riches in savings and loan companies, whilst mummy starves on her pension. So, if you're a bit tight and inclined to be very careful about what and how you give, serve this economical dish to your fastidious folks.

## Oxtail Ragoût

2 or 3 packages of oxtails
1 can of oxtail soup
1 large onion, sliced
6 - 8 carrots, sliced thickly
4 leeks
1 cup of bouillon
1 clove of garlic
1 tsp. thyme
salt and pepper
2 tbsp. butter

Brown the oxtails quickly in hot butter or margarine until they are well browned all over. Turn down the heat and add to the pan the sliced onions, two thickly sliced carrots, the chopped garlic clove and salt and pepper to taste. Sauté for a few minutes until the vegetables are seasoned and slightly wilted.

Then add the oxtail soup, 1 cup of bouillon and the thyme and cook slowly over a low heat for an hour and a half or longer. About 40 minutes before serving add the remaining carrots and the sliced leeks (which you must wash thoroughly in order to remove all the grit). If the sauce thickens too much, you can add some broth or water as it cooks.

This dish is usually served with a potato purée or with broad, flat noodles. A nice accompanyment is a salad of romaine lettuce with thin strips of pickled beets, rings of mild red onions, green Bell pepper and French or Italian dressing.

Serves 4.

# Anxiety

A persistent feeling of dread, apprehension or impending disaster is symptomatic of anxiety. Anxiety differs from fear in not being referable to a specific object or event, and is often misused in colloquial terms. If you are fussing lest your turkey turn out dry — you are fearful, not anxious. While you are likely to be "eager" to please (not anxious), if your houseguests lackadaisically mumble something about having "all the time in the world," it might indeed behoove you to be "afraid" to please. But, again, not anxious.

Now, if you are afraid of everything or nothing, then you're anxious.

If you are slightly terrified that your tapioca will turn out lumpy — no, that's not it — well, perhaps it's because your crepe suzettes might catch fire — no that's not it either. But if your mouth is dry, palms are wet, heart is pounding, lungs are panting, and you feel faint, you are correctly anxious and may pace a few times through the house before trying this dish.

## Pork Chops Piquant

4 thick pork chops
fine bread crumbs
4 tbsp. butter or margarine
1 clove garlic, minced
1 tbsp. prepared mustard
1 tsp. dry mustard
1 tsp. Worcestershire sauce
¼ tsp. dill weed
2 tbsp. dill pickles, finely chopped
1 scant tbsp. flour
½ cup chicken broth or bouillon
½ cup sherry or white wine
salt and pepper

In a heavy skillet, heat 1 tablespoon of butter and brown the chops quickly on both sides. Then cover the pan, turn the heat down to medium-low and cook the chops for 20 minutes. When the chops are nearly done remove them from the skillet and place them on an oven-proof serving dish after pressing them firmly in the fine bread crumbs. Dot them with a little butter and place them in a medium oven while you prepare the sauce. Keep the pan juices as they will be used later.

In a saucepan combine 2 tbsp. of butter, the minced garlic clove and both the mustards. Stir and cook gently over a low heat. Then add the dill, salt and pepper and the Worcestershire sauce.

Using the skillet that you cooked the chops in, reheat the pan juices adding 1 tbsp. of butter. Then add the flour to make a thickened roux. To this you add the sherry and the broth and cook over a medium heat, stirring constantly. This sauce should not be too thick. To it add the chopped pickles and the mustard sauce. Serve the chops on a platter with the piquant sauce on the side.

The chops are tasty and an unusual approach to pork chops so don't let the pickles in the recipe make you anxious.

Serves 4.

# Blocking

Blocking is a momentary disturbance in the thought processes. Conceptual progressions, normally quite clear, may suddenly cease and the consciousness "goes blank." This phenomenon occurs especially when an individual is under stress and is probably caused by subliminal activity associated with unpleasant emotion, such as anxiety or conflict.

The reasons for blocking are varied but the process often involves some shutting down of memory circuits due to conflict back at the power station, so to speak. Suddenly forgetting your wife's name when introducing her to your new secretary is an example. Leaving one of the children, perhaps the one whose advent caused you to give up your career as a ballerina, at the railroad station, say, in Saskatoon and forgetting to pick him up might also be an exhibition of this little mechanism.

If you are conflicted about fish and tend to block out recipes for them, you can work out a rather nice personal psychotherapy by trying this menu.

## Sole Fouquet

4 large fillets sole or 8 small fillets
1 bay leaf
1 small onion (sliced fine)
2 cups water
thyme
salt and pepper
pinch of tarragon

## Sauce

3 tbsp. butter
3 tbsp. flour
½ cup wine (white, dry)
½ cup sliced mushrooms
2 tbsp. Parmesan cheese
1 tbsp. tomato paste
1 cup bottled clam juice (optional)

Put the sole fillets in a shallow baking dish, add water, onions, bay leaf, thyme, salt and pepper, and tarragon. Use the tarragon very sparingly as you want only a hint of this seasoning, not a full orchestration. Simmer the fish for a few minutes, until it is done and then pour off and keep the liquid from it. Strain it – or remove the bay leaf – and prepare the sauce while keeping the sole warm.

For the sauce, first cook the mushrooms in butter. Sauté them until done, then add the flour. Mix in the liquid from the fish, or you may substitute the clam juice if you prefer. Cook this until it is thick. If it needs thinning add a little white wine.

Then add to this sauce the Parmesan cheese, tomato paste, white wine, and salt and pepper.
Pour the sauce over the fish and place it under the broiler very briefly until it browns. Serve hot, bubbling and delicious.

Serve with wild rice pilaf and a green vegetable.

Serves 4.

# Bruxism

The condition of bruxism refers to abnormal habits of chewing, such as the persistent grinding of teeth. This grinding may continue during sleep and often produces pain in the jaw. Pathological masticators are often overly dependent individuals, expressing much hostility. To avoid harmful wear and tear on molars and mandibles, try gnashing and gnawing on some gnocchi, or these tasty bones.

**Stuffed Spareribs**

4 - 5 lbs. spareribs
½ cup mushrooms, chopped
1 stalk of celery, chopped
1 tsp. tumeric
½ tsp. sage
butter or margarine
2 cups bread crumbs
1 medium onion, chopped
1 egg
½ tsp. thyme
salt and pepper

Cut the ribs in slabs of 5-6 ribs or leave in long strips. Season them with salt and pepper.

In a skillet sauté the onions, celery and mushrooms until partially cooked. In a bowl, combine the bread crumbs, egg, and seasonings, and mix them together thoroughly. To the bread, add the chopped sautéed vegetables and mix them well. If it is too dry, add a little melted butter.

Stuff the spareribs with the dressing. If the ribs are in long strips, spread the stuffing along the inside of the ribs, roll them up and tie them with twine. If they are too thick for that, cut them into smaller slabs, putting stuffing between 2 sections of ribs; tie them and bake in a 350° oven until well done. Brush the ribs two or three times with a little melted butter or margarine if they seem dry.

Use a roaster with a rack as there is a lot of fat on ribs. These ribs are filling, and are best served with some fairly light dishes such as tomato, cucumber, and lettuce with wine, vinegar and/or salad dressing.

Serves 4.

# Castration Anxiety

This is (primarily) a male complaint, so, herewith, are a few notes for the male chef. First of all, you will want to stay away from cleavers, cutters, sharp knives, and better chefs. The best approach for you is to make a specialty of soups, pancakes, desserts, or cocktails. Just forget all those times the family told you you'd never be half the man your father was, and cook up a grand assortment of phallic symbols such as:

**Stuffed Zucchini with Father's Frankfurters**

4 large zucchini squash
1 small carton sour cream
2 large sliced tomatoes
dill weed
4 large frankfurters
8 strips bacon
8 slices cheddar cheese
½ cup barbecue sauce

Boil the zucchini squash whole until it is almost done but still slightly firmer than the finished product. When it is almost done, remove it from the pan and split it part way through. Then spoon over the sour cream and add the slices of tomato and a dash of dill on each squash. Place in an oven with the broiler rack about three-quarters of the way up the oven and broil until the cream is bubbling.

For the franks, fry the bacon until it is about half done. Slice open the franks and place in them the cheese rolled into cylinders and the barbecue sauce. Wrap the bacon slices around each frank. Broil for a few minutes until the cheese is melted and the bacon is done.

Serves 2-4, depending on the anxiety level of the diners.

# Catalepsy & Stereotypy

A constantly maintained immobility of body position is known as catalepsy. Stereotypy is when a specific motion or activity is initiated, then repeated for an indefinite period. Both catalepsy and stereotypy are advantageous conditions in the otherwise tedious preparation of this delicious sauce. In culinary terms, the necessary process is phrased as: "stand still and stir" for what seems an interminable length of time. In the midst of all the standing and stirring, your mind may wander and you may begin to question it all. In these critical hours, it sometimes helps to envision yourself as a kind of Tableau Vivant.

**Boring Bearnaise**

This recipe combines two sauces and the ingredients will be listed separately.

*Hollandaise*

¼ lb. butter
2 tsp. lemon juice
3 egg yolks
½ tsp. salt

*Bearnaise*

1 tsp. dried tarragon
2 tsp. chopped green onion
2 tsp. chopped parsley
3 tbsp. white avine vinegar
1 tbsp. water

To make the Bearnaise, cook the tarragon, parsley, and onions in the water mixed with the vinegar until they are cooked almost to a glaze. Set this aside and make the Hollandaise.

Use a double boiler and heat water in the lower section. In the top half put the butter and melt it, stirring slowly. Lightly beat the egg yolks and add in the lemon juice and salt as you do. Add the yolks to the butter but do not let the water in the bottom half come to a boil. Continue lightly beating and cooking until the sauce thickens.

Add the Bearnaise base to the Hollandaise and continue beating until it is thick.

This can be served with a variety of meat and vegetable dishes, but is especially nice with white fish.

# Catatonia

A person who has become catatonic has severely withdrawn from reality. He is usually mute, immobile, and unresponsive. Although this is a serious state of withdrawal, the incidence of spontaneous recovery is very high. The catatonic isolation may last for days, even months, but the long-term prognosis is good.

One of the most dramatic of all psychotic conditions, catatonia is notable for the silence and stupor.

Although the individual appears to be totally "out-of-touch" with his environment, he is generally able to accurately describe those surroundings after his recovery. When in the catatonic state, the person will stare fixedly, remain in whatever postural position he is placed, and be uncommunicatively mute in the face of all attempts to rouse him. There is an element of hostility in this profound withdrawal into a very thick defensive shell. In a sense, it becomes the ultimate technique in the interpersonal rebuff of "ignoring."

### Clam Chowder

1 quart of clams (ground or chopped)
3 oz. salt pork
1 onion, chopped
4 potatoes, diced
½ cup leeks, sliced
¼ cup celery, chopped
1½ pints milk
salt and pepper
butter
1 small bay leaf
½ tsp. thyme
water

Slowly sauté the salt pork until golden. Remove. To the pan add the onions and celery and sauté until wilted. Add the potatoes, leeks, and the juice from the clams. Cover this with boiling water and let it cook slowly until the potatoes are done. Add the herbs, seasonings, and the clams and cook for another 15 minutes. Just before serving, heat the milk and add it to the chowder, along with a good sized lump of butter.

This is nice served with a large raw spinach salad with red onion rings, cucumber slices, and French dressing. A platter of hot toast rings or crisp toasted muffins is a good addition.

# Claustrophobia

Claustrophobia is the unfounded fear of small, enclosed, or crowded places. A person with claustrophobia is an ideal candidate for the Foreign Legion but should steer clear of the Submarine Service and class reunions. (Whenever possible, he should seek the coveted office of Dalai Lama.) The claustrophobe cannot tolerate several other humans in close proximity to his person, and therefore while shopping in the supermarket should always wear a hula hoop. The following recipe is suggested because one can be quite free and relatively unfettered in selecting the amounts of various ingredients, and after consuming this chili-peppered dish, one will probably not be surrounded by interpersonal demands for intimacy.

**Chili Con Queso**

½ lb. process cheese
½ lb. cheddar cheese
2 or 3 small yellow hot chili peppers
1 onion
2 cloves of garlic
1 can tomatoes, large

Sauté the chopped onion and garlic with the diced chili peppers. When browned, add the tomatoes and let simmer for about 15 minutes. Then add the cut up cheeses and let it all simmer until the cheese is thoroughly melted.

This is a colourful hot dip and is most delicious served with tortillas or corn chips and a light red or rosé wine.

# Compulsive Overeating

Most of us overeat at least some time, but some of us are driven to excessive consumption all the time. This may be related to deep-rooted feelings of insecurity, with the taking in of food symbolizing the taking in of love. Thus, if you love to eat, you may eat for love. But compulsive eating often destroys the real pleasure of food and reduces the joy, if not the waistline. I would recommend overstuffing the food instead of overstuffing yourself, which will satisfy your compulsion to cram while relieving the strain on your digestive tract.

### Overstuffed Mushrooms

8 large mushrooms
⅔ cup fine bread crumbs
1 egg
1 tsp. turmeric
2 tbsp. minced onion
salt and pepper
margarine or butter

Buy the largest mushrooms you can find. Wash them and remove the stems. Set the caps aside, and chop the stems finely.

In a bowl combine the fine bread crumbs, egg, a little minced onion, the chopped stems, and the seasonings. Mix well. If too dry, add just a little water or some melted butter. Fill the mushroom caps with the mixture. Place caps top down on a buttered baking dish and bake in a moderate oven about 20 minutes. Brush with melted butter to keep them moist.

These mushrooms make a very nice vegetable side dish with fish or meat that is served with a sauce.

2 per person.

# Cyclothymic Personality

Cyclothymic personalities are identified by an outgoing adjustment to life and a ready enthusiasm for competition. But moods alternate frequently between elation and sadness, and cyclothymic people are on an emotional roller-coaster. In cheerful, vivacious moods, a cyclothymic will take on difficult tasks with energy and boundless enthusiasm, but depression often follows. This Spanish dish is marvellous for the "high" period as it requires a dauntless approach to shopping and preparation – and it is well worth the effort, so if you're on the "up"-swing, seek out the following ingredients and dash around the kitchen in exhilaration, making:

**Paella**

1 lb. lobster, cooked
1 lb. shrimp, cooked and shelled
1 doz. small clams
1 qt. mussels
1 lb. chicken, cut-up
1 tsp. oregano
½ tsp. coriander
1 tsp. capers
1 chorizo sausage, sliced, or
    small mild salami
6 tbsps. Olive oil
1 tsp. vinegar
1 onion (chopped)
2 peppercorns
1 clove of garlic (minced)
1 tbsp. salt
1 oz. salt pork (chopped)
3 tbsp. tomato sauce
1 package frozen peas
1 can pimento, small
2¼ cups uncooked, long grain rice
4 cups boiling water
1 tsp. saffron

Remove the meat from the lobster. Shell and devein the shrimp. Scrub the clams and mussels. Cut the chicken into large bite-size pieces. Combine the oregano, peppercorns, garlic, salt, olive oil, and vinegar and mash it all with a spoon. Rub the chicken with this mixture.

Heat olive oil in a deep, heavy skillet and brown the chicken lightly over a moderate heat. Add the chorizo, salt pork, onions, coriander, and capers. Cook 10 minutes over a low heat. Then add the tomato sauce and rice and cook another 5 minutes.

Add the boiling water, saffron and shrimps. Mix well and cook rapidly until the liquid is absorbed. This should take about 20 minutes. With a large wooden spoon, turn the mixture so that the rice mixes well with the rest of the ingredients. Add the lobster meat and peas, cover and cook 5 minutes. Steam the mussels and clams in a little water until the shells open. Heat the pimentoes.

Serve the paella on a large preheated plate and put the mussels, clams, and pimentoes generously on the top for colour as well as flavour.

After you've gone through all this, your euphoric stage should diminish and you can stave off a post-supper mild depression knowing you have served a wonderful and rare treat.

Serves 6-8.

# Electra or Oedipus Complex

Oedipus was a mythological young man who loved his mother, not wisely, but too well. The Oedipus complex refers to the attachment that young boys have to their mothers and the resulting conflicts that end up with wanting "a girl just like the girl that married dear old dad." The Electra complex is the same system for girls and their fathers. Electra or Oedipus: bring back the good old days of mother love with —

**Mom's Lemon Pie**

1¼ cup sugar
1½ cup warm water
1 tbsp. butter
4 tbsp. cornstarch
3 tbsp. cold water
6 tbsp. lemon juice
1 tsp. grated lemon rind
2 tbsp. thick cream
3 egg yolks
1 precooked pastry shell

*Meringue*

3 egg whites
¼ cup sugar

Combine the sugar and butter in a double boiler and heat with the warm water until the sugar dissolves.

Add the cornstarch which has been blended with the cold water. Cook slowly until clear (about 8 minutes). Then add the lemon juice and rind and cook for 2 minutes. Add the egg yolks beaten lightly with cream. Bring it to a boil and then remove from heat and pour it into an 8-inch pastry shell.

Cool the pie and spread with meringue made by beating the separated egg whites and a few drops of vanilla until the whites are stiff. Add ¼ cup of sugar as you are beating them. The meringue may be lightly browned before serving, if desired.

# Euphoria

Euphoria refers to an overly pleasant emotional condition or mood. A euphoric person is imbued with a sense of well-being and assurance. He or she has a marked air of self-confidence, and radiates enjoyment often unrelated to any particular life circumstance. These are the type of people (often seen on television) who just seem to get a greater bang out of switching deodorants than either you or me. They gravitate toward certain occupations, the ladies as Stewardesses, the men as M.C.'s for talk-shows with children under six. So if your husband works for a man called "Smilin' " anybody, and he's coming to dinner, the best solution is to strive for group euphoria. This pleasurable mood can be closely imitated by imbibing liberally the following concoction. Enjoy.

**Sangria Elan**

2 bottles *dry* white wine or
    sparkling white wine
1 bottle dry red wine
½ bottle 7-Up or ginger ale
2 large oranges
2 lemons
1 lime
½ box, clean, sliced strawberries
2 fresh sliced peaches

Mix the wines together in a punch bowl, add the 7-Up, and let it sit. Cut up the citrus fruit into wedges and squeeze them into the wines. Drop the other fruit slices into the wines, add ice cubes, and put in refrigerator to chill. Serve with a highly spiced dip, such as chili con quesco (see page 32) and corn chips.

This Spanish libation can also be made with champagne instead of white wine.

It's a wonderful punch, but tends to sneak up on you, so when you've reached the proper state of euphoria, slacken off on the sangria and head for the chip dip.

# Exhibitionism

Exhibitionism is a need to expose oneself, to the delight or horror of others. There are varying degrees of exhibitionism and varying degrees of audience appreciation. The element of surprise is important to the exhibitionist, popping up and out at unexpected moments. People often ask, "What is the proper thing to say in such circumstances?" A simple "Hi, there" is probably sufficient.

If you like the southern exposure, take off your apron and try –

40

## Rump Round

1½ lbs. round or rump
2 tbsp. butter
1 small green bell pepper (chopped)
1 large onion
½ lb. mushrooms
½ cup sherry
6 carrots, diced
thyme
parsley
onion salt
pepper
1 tbsp. flour
1 bay leaf

Drench thin strips or small chunks of round steak in flour, and brown in butter until thoroughly seared on all sides. Add the onions and sauté briefly. Remove the meat and onions and add the sherry to the pan. Simmer and stir the sherry and meat glaze. Put meat, onions, diced carrots, green pepper, mushrooms, and seasonings back in the pan and simmer for 45 minutes. Add a little more sherry or beef broth if necessary. Remove bay leaf before serving.

Serves 4.

Serve with boiled potatoes and parsley and an asparagus salad.

Or, you might try the following mashed potato balls for an attractive accompaniment.

## Orange Potato Balls

potatoes for 4 people
½ cup cheddar cheese, cut into strips
butter or margarine
1 egg yolk, beaten
1 tbsp. grated orange rind
¾ cup milk or sour cream
salt and pepper

Peel and boil the potatoes until well cooked. Then put them through a ricer or beat them with an electric mixer until smooth. While beating the potatoes, add milk, butter, grated orange rind, and salt and pepper according to taste.

After they are beaten, but not too creamy, let them cool, then mould them into medium-sized balls and cover each potato ball with strips of cheddar cheese. Beat the egg yolk and brush the yolk over the potatoes so that they will be golden when baked. Pop them in a medium oven for 10-15 minutes or until golden.

# Fetishism

Fetishes are objects or situations which a person associates with sex and which are sexually arousing. Fetishes are very individualistic and are whatever turns you on. In selecting a fetish, one can be as imaginative and creative as one chooses. For you chefs, your fetish need not be thy lady's garter, it could be your granny's antimacassar. Fetishists are more likely to be male than female, so ladies often find themselves confronted with hubby's favourites. So, if your husband is super passionate only when clad in his rainboots, try serving him eggs benedict in one of his galoshes. Or, if he has the more common breast fetish, offer up this menu.

## Bosom de Poulet

4 double breasts of chicken
2 tbsp. sherry or marsala
1 tsp. ketchup
1 tbsp. flour
½ cup stock (chicken)
1½ cups sour cream
1 tbsp. currant jelly
1 tbsp. grated Parmesan cheese
4 tbsp. butter
2 cups mushrooms
dash of cayenne pepper
1 tbsp. dill weed

Bone the breasts and dust them with flour, then brown them in butter and pour the wine over them. Remove the chicken and add the tomato ketchup and flour to the pan. Stir in the stock.

Stir until the mixture blends and thickens and then slowly add the sour cream. Season with the jelly and cheese and the salt and pepper. Put back the chicken breasts, cover the pan and cook gently for 20 minutes.

When done, remove the breasts and arrange them on an ovenproof platter, pour the sauce and some Parmesan cheese over them, and run them under the broiler to brown.

Slice the mushrooms and sauté them in hot butter and add a dash of cayenne pepper. Cook briskly for 3 to 4 minutes, add a dash of sherry and dill. Serve these on top of the chicken.

Lettuce wedges topped with rings of sweet red onions and French dressing and a rice dish complete this menu.

Serves 4.

# Flagellant

A flagellant is a person who derives sensual pleasure from simulated or actual beating or lashing. Just standing around whipping cream can make the day for the true flagellant. So, if someone says they like your long lashes, watch for the undertones.

**Baked Flank Steak Flagellata**

1 good size flank steak
½ cup mushrooms (chopped)
3 oz. pâté or liver sausage
½ cup red wine
½ tsp. dry mustard
salt and pepper

Lay out the flank steak and beat it vigorously with a mallet or heavy knife handle. This will break down the fibres and make the steak tender. Then marinate it in the wine for an hour or so.

Just before putting it in a moderate oven, cover the inside of the steak with the pâté or liver sausage which has been seasoned with mustard and salt and pepper. Sprinkle the top with chopped mushrooms and roll up the steak. Place it on a rack in a roasting pan, pour over the wine marinade, and bake for 30 to 40 minutes.

# Frigidity

Frigidity is a condition of inhibited sexual response occurring in some ladies from time to time. So in those moods when you are more moved to move around in the kitchen than the bedroom, this production should bring about a pleasurable response.

**Cold Broccoli Rémoulade**

1 large bunch of fresh broccoli
1 cup mayonnaise
2 cloves chopped garlic
1 tsp. dry mustard
1 chopped boiled egg
½ tsp. tarragon
salt and pepper
1 tbsp. chopped parsley

Cook the broccoli by plunging it into fiercely boiling water for 8 to 10 minutes. North Americans tend to overcook vegetables which makes them watery and tasteless. Bringing the water to a rolling boil first helps to avoid this. As soon as the broccoli is done, remove it from the water, place in a collander to cool, and then put it in the refrigerator to chill.

Mix together the mayonnaise, mustard, tarragon, chopped garlic, egg, and salt and pepper. Chill this also. When ready to serve, arrange the broccoli on a platter with the sauce on the side.

This is a very good vegetable dish to serve with fried chicken or a simple beef roast.

# Gilles de la Tourette Syndrome

This is a relatively rare phenomenon, indicating an individual's tendency to bark obscenities compulsively and out of context. To distinguish this syndrome from the cries of the oppressed young or the inebriated old, it must be specifically applied to uncontrollable, intermittent outbursts. The phenomenon can be thought of as a verbal tic, in the sense that the obscene utterances are unintentional and without conscious volition. Thus, if occasional epithets emerge from the kitchen, the crucial question diagnostically is whether or not it would happen if the cook were in: the PTA meeting, the supermarket, or the front pew.

**Four-Letter Veal (or pork)**

1 breast of veal or pork
1 medium onion, diced
½ cup mushrooms, diced
3 tbsp. butter
2 tbsp. flour
½ cup sherry
½ cup milk
4 ounces swiss cheese, diced
pinch of thyme
pinch of celery seed
salt and pepper

Sauté the onions and mushrooms in one tbsp. butter until they are partially cooked. Cut the breast in two (lengthwise), season with salt and pepper, and spread the sautéed onions and mushrooms over the meat.

In a heavy-bottomed saucepan melt the two remaining tbsp. butter and add the flour. Blend well and then slowly add the sherry. Stir, remove from the heat, and add the milk.

Return to a low heat and stir, adding the thyme and celery seed. (If the sauce is too thick, add more milk but it should not be thinned down too much.) Then add the diced swiss cheese and stir until it is melted. Pour the sauce over the meat and bake in a 350° oven 50-60 minutes, or until done.

Serve with tiny whole parslied new potatoes and zucchini, seasoned with butter, dill, and parsley.

This is a rich dish and the meat goes a long way, consequently, allow ½ lb. of lean pork per person.

A nice dessert for this dish would be strawberries marinated in Kirsch and a little sugar and served with plain cookies.

# Grandiosity

Delusions of grandeur generally develop as overcompensation for the individual's deep feelings of inferiority. By the assumption of a powerful and famous identity, it becomes possible to consciously deny one's own inadequacies.

World figures, past or present, often serve as models for this "identity-stealing," and the grandiose person tends to select a particular king, artist, explorer or priest, symbolizing his own area of fear and fantasy.

If one were indeed Richard I, one could not have just lost the Lions' Club election; nor would Nijinsky have realized, halfway through the dance, that he was fox-trotting to a waltz.

A touch of madness becomes us all and your personal majesty or courage can be nicely expressed through Crown of Ribs.

## Crown Ribs of Lamb

4-5 lbs. lamb ribs
2 cups beef bouillon
1 tbsp. chives
1 tbsp. buttter
1 cup dry rice
1 onion, minced
strips of salt pork

Take the rib rack and cut between the bones, but don't cut all the way through. Clean the ribs, turn the meat inward and fasten it so that it forms a ring. Put this crown of ribs in a roasting pan, dab it with butter, and lay some strips of salt pork across the top for self-basting.

Roast the ribs in a 350° oven for about 35 minutes, basting frequently.

Meanwhile, back at the rice: place the raw rice, minced onion, and chives in a bit of butter in a sauce pan and sauté for a few minutes. This will brown the rice slightly and partially cook the onions and chives. Then pour in the 2 cups of beef broth, bring to a boil, cover tightly and turn down to a very low heat for 15 minutes. This rice pilaf is then served by placing it in the centre of the crown of ribs.

Serves 4 (Usually allow 1 lb. per person.)

Lamb is good served with fruit, so you might like to try the following. Take 1 canned peach half per person, place a teaspoon of butter in the centres and sprinkle with cinnamon. Run them under the broiler until the butter melts with the seasoning and the peach half is heated. Serve hot.

The following celery root recipe is also a good side dish.

### Celeriac (Celery Root)

After peeling a celery root, slice it and boil for a few minutes. When it is tender, remove it from the water and put the slices on an oven-proof platter. Sprinkle grated Parmesan or Romano cheese over the celery root, dot with butter, and run under the broiler for a few minutes.

# Group Therapy

This is a currently popular type of treatment which takes many different forms and uses a wide variety of approaches. Any group can be therapeutic and/or analytic, so here are some tips on doing it yourself at your next fondue group. The basic equipment is 1 pot, several forks, and food to be cooked individually but with group co-operation.

Look for:
– the facilitator, the person who passes out the forks and makes sure everybody has enough elbow room.
– the information giver who tells you things like "your meat fell on the floor."
– the procrastinator who gets everything arranged on his plate before cooking it and by then it's too late.
– the id-ridden frantic who grabs anyone's fork and/or scrapes madly about picking up pieces that have fallen off a neighbour's fork.
– the anxious phobic who won't let go of his fork *ever* for fear it will get mixed up with someone else's fork.

– the hostile type who sneers in the midst of it all, "Oh, a salad as well? How generous."
– the competitive fighter who insists that the one that's done is his.
– the pyromaniac who keeps eyeing the Sterno and calling for a higher flame.

Identifying your own and others' behaviour in a group is a major focus of this method. And, if all goes well, there should be a group resolution with a finale of naked forks in a circle and everyone casting aside inhibitions and crying that they don't care whose fork it is – it's beautiful!

## Fondue

cubes of lean beef and veal
cauliflowerets
oil for cooking

## Sauces

*Hot Mustard*

2 tbsp. butter
2 tbsp. finely chopped onion
2 tbsp. flour
1 cup whole milk
tabasco
2 tsp. dry mustard
2 tbsp. prepared mustard
2 tbsp. brown sugar
water

Sauté onions in the butter until tender. Stir in the flour and cook slowly for a few minutes. Add the milk and cook and stir until it is a smooth sauce. Season with salt, pepper, and a few drops of tabasco. Mix 2 tsp. of dry mustard to a paste by adding a very little bit of water and then mix this into the prepared mustard and the brown sugar. Stir this into the sauce and blend until it is smooth. Bring it to a boil then take it off the heat and strain it through a sieve. Serve hot.

*Bearnaise*

2 egg yolks
1 tbsp. tarragon vinegar
2 tbsp. cream
1 tsp. chopped chives
4 tbsp. butter
1 tsp. fresh tarragon *or*
¼ tsp. dried tarragon
1 tsp. fresh parsley, chopped
salt and pepper
cayenne, a few grains

Mix egg yolks, vinegar, cream, salt and pepper in bowl on top of double boiler. Place pot over saucepan of hot water over slow fire; stir with a whisk until the mixture begins to thicken. Add the butter, bit by bit, then the tarragon, parsley, and cayenne and chives. Blend.

*Curry*

2 tbsp. butter
¼ cup onion, finely chopped
¾ apple, peeled, cored, and cubed
2 tbsp. flour
1 tbsp. curry powder
1 cup milk, scalded
salt
2 tbsp. peanut butter

Melt the butter and sauté in the onions and apple until they are tender. Sprinkle with a mixture of flour and curry powder. Blend it all well and gradually add the milk. Then add salt and the peanut butter. Cook this all over a low heat stirring constantly until the sauce is thick and smooth.

53

# Hypochondriasis

This syndrome is a fairly common one and refers to the neurotic tendency to become fearfully concerned about physical health and illness. The true hypochondriac enlarges upon any physical ills he or she may have and tends to worry about ones that haven't even appeared yet. But many people, when under stress and tension, tend to focus their diffuse anxiety upon real and imagined illness, to the distress of relatives and the enrichment of general practitioners. Most of us have the need to regale folks with tales of our last operation; the hypochondriac will hold you spellbound as he chronicles his latest observation that he's had two attacks of the hiccups in the last month, which the specialist will undoubtedly establish as being due to the same disease process which has caused him to drink much more than his usual amounts of mineral water this past week. Or perhaps, about the time when he thought his epiglottis had atrophied.

Short of total committment to a health food diet, perhaps the best way to handle your Hypochondriasis is to buy only the freshest meats, vegetables, wash everything thoroughly and cook it all quickly. That way no lurking ptomaine or pesticides will invade your soma and disturb your psyche. (This recipe provides prunes, which can add a healthy boost to your digestive tract.)

## Casserole Santé

2 onions, sliced
1 bay leaf
2 sprigs parsley
½ lemon, sliced
1 fresh beef tongue
½ cup tarragon vinegar
½ cup red wine
½ cup sugar
¼ tsp. ground cloves
¼ tsp. cinnamon
½ cup seedless raisins
1 cup soaked pitted prunes
1 tbsp. salt
1 tbsp. butter
1 tsp. flour
pepper
(¼ cup blanched almonds are optional)

Wash the tongue thoroughly, place it in a large, heavy casserole and cover it with cold water. Then add the onions, parsley, lemon, bay leaf, salt and pepper. This should be simmered for between 2 to 3 hours, depending on the size of the tongue. As long as it feels hard when tested with a fork, it isn't done. When it is done, remove it and skin it and then replace it and let it cool in the broth in which it was cooked.

In a sauce pan, melt the butter and add the flour until it blends. Then add the vinegar and red wine until it thickens. The sugar is then added along with the cinnamon and cloves.

To this sauce is then added the raisins and prunes until they are heated and blended. (The almonds, if used, also go into the sauce at this point.) The broth is then drained from the tongue and reserved for later use if you want to add liquid to the sauce.

Pour the sauce over the tongue and simmer very slowly for 30 minutes, basting often. When serving, carve into thin, even slices and cover liberally with sauce.

Serve with a rice pilaf cooked in beef broth instead of water and cucumber salad.

# Hysteria

Contrary to popular language and belief, hysteria does *not* refer to the state in which you found yourself halfway through the viewing of "Psycho." Hysteria is, technically, a neurotic syndrome which is characterized by emotional changeability, coquettishness, the tendency to dramatize, and a rather "Pollyanna-ish" approach to problems. Hysterics are generally partial to pastel coloured gloves, adore hydrangias, and hate Ingmar Bergman. If this describes the real you, don your best pink apron and create this frothy "it-will-all-be-better-after-supper" dessert.

**Strawberry Glee**

16 marshmallows
1 cup milk
1 pkg. lemon jello
2 three oz. pkgs. cream cheese
1 pkg. fresh frozen strawberries
1 cup cream
⅔ cup mayonnaise

In a double boiler melt the marshmallows and the milk. When blended, pour the hot mixture over the gelatin in a large bowl. Stir until it is dissolved, cut in the cream cheese and stir it until cheese blends and melts. Then add the thawed strawberries and the cream and mayonnaise. Chill until firm.

# Impotence

Many men find themselves impotent at one time or another throughout their lives. They seem to be more drastically upset by this often temporary condition than are their wives. If a man begins to fear he has lost all sexual prowess, this can become a self-fulfilling prophecy. The best approach is to maintain a calm perspective. While the condition lasts, fussing won't help; console yourself with this dessert that *does* rise.

### Impotence Soufflé

2 tbsp. butter
¾ cup milk
1 lemon (juice and grated rind)
5 egg whites
3 level tbsp. flour
4 tbsp. sugar
4 egg yolks

Melt the butter in a saucepan and blend in the flour until thoroughly mixed, then slowly add the milk. Stir the mixture slowly until it is smooth and thick. Add the juice of one lemon and the grated lemon rind.

Beat the egg whites until they are stiff. Lightly beat the 4 egg yolks separately, add the sugar and blend this into the sauce. Lastly, fold in the beaten egg whites.

Grease a soufflé dish and dust it with sugar. French chefs usually tie waxed paper around the outside to form a cuff. Pour the lemon mixture into the dish and bake for 15 minutes in a 350° oven.

Remove the paper and serve at once.

Serves 4.

# Inhibition

Inhibition refers to the control of emotional impulses and sexual feelings. An inhibited person is proper, polite, genteel, and well censored. If modesty is your meat and you have a tendency to knock on the oven door before opening it, you'll love this well-covered dish.

**Pardon-me Pork**

1 pork rib roast
½ cup molasses
1 tsp. dry mustard
3 tbsp. ketchup
2 tbsp. vinegar
½ cup red wine
pinch of ginger
salt and pepper

Stand the roast on a rack in a roaster or casserole dish. Season with salt and pepper and cook at 375° for 30 minutes. Turn the oven down to 325°. Spoon off excess fat. Mix the molasses with the other ingredients and pour half of this sauce over the roast.

About 20 minutes before the roast is done, pour over the remainder of the sauce.

Cook it covered.

Serve this flavourful pork with tiny new potatoes and cooked carrots modestly covered with dill.

Serves 4.

# Kleptomania

Kleptomania is an overwhelming compulsion to steal, and is generally a female symptom. Freudian theory equates the urge to steal objects with the urge to steal love, and posits personal insecurities as the root cause. The true kleptomaniac steals items which are not essential to her, and she usually could well afford to pay for them.

The banker's wife caught on the curb outside the supermarket with a watermelon tucked in her girdle probably suffers from this syndrome.

Stealing recipes is a less punishable and far more palatable past-time. Leave this on your stove for a sick friend to snitch.

## Tournedos Rossini

filet steaks
large fresh mushrooms
onion powder
1 can pâté de foie
salt and pepper
1 tbsp. butter

Season the steaks on both sides with the salt, pepper, and onion powder. Sear them quickly in a hot pan and butter, and then slide them under the broiler and cook for several minutes on each side. Spread the pâté on one side of the steaks and slip them back under the broiler.

In the pan in which the steaks were seared, place the large mushroom caps and sauté them until cooked. Just before serving the steaks, place two mushrooms on each one and let them broil very briefly.

These tasty steaks are complimented by cooked fresh or frozen asparagus served with a Hollandaise sauce and toasted garlic bread.

## Potato and Dill Soup

4 large potatoes (peeled and sliced)
1½ cups water or chicken bouillon
1 cup milk
½ tsp. dill weed
salt and pepper
1 small bunch of leeks
½ tsp. dry mustard
chopped parsley
3 tbsp. flour
3 tbsp. butter

Melt the butter in a sauce pan, add the flour and blend well. Chop in the leeks and potatoes and mix the vegetables thoroughly with the butter and flour paste. Then add slowly the milk and the water, the mustard, dill weed, salt and pepper. Cook slowly until the potatoes are done and then, using a masher, crush the potatoes and leeks so that the soup becomes thick. Simmer.

Before serving this potage, sprinkle each helping with the chopped parsley.

# Masochism

Masochism is a form of erotic enjoyment wherein the person obtains pleasure from experiencing pain. A masochist likes to be hurt, and at crowded cocktail parties will never ever say, "Pardon me, but you're standing on my foot." He'll just smile, silently. Those of you who have been tied to a hot stove every day will no doubt be familiar with this phenomenon of joyous agony. If you wish to increase your pain, you might try inviting your in-laws and employers for the following impressive delicacy. This particular dish has marvellous advantages for the masochist, in that it takes a long time to prepare and can turn out to be an utter failure. So I would suggest that you begin in a tiny kitchen without air-conditioning sometime in July — a fifth-floor Toronto apartment would do, or a travel trailer in a Texas backyard.

And, happily enough, many hours later, your crust may crumble into little flaky pieces. However, if your will to fail fails, you just might succeed in creating this marvellous dinner-party dish.

**Sufferers' Roast Wellington**

*Roast*

3½ - 4 lb.- boneless roast of beef
1 cup ground ham
1 cup ground mushrooms
2 or 3 tbsp. sherry or white wine
½ tsp. marjoram or rosemary
¼ tsp. dry mustard

*Crust*

2½ cups flour, sifted
1 tsp. salt
12 tbsp. shortening
3 or 4 tbsp. ice water
2 egg yolks (beaten)

Buy a good beef roast with no bone; a sirloin tip or eye of round will do nicely. Season it and let it set while you prepare the outer layers. Grind up the ham and mushrooms in a grinder and add 2 tbsp. sherry or white wine. Season this with salt and pepper, a dash of dry mustard, and a little marjoram or rosemary. Make a paste of this mixture and pat it all around the roast like an icing.

Prepare a crust for the outer layer. Into a bowl, sift the flour and salt. Add the butter or shortening and blend it with your fingertips until it is mealy. Then add 3 or 4 tbsp. of water and blend the dough. Roll the dough in wax paper and leave it in the refrigerator for 15-20 minutes. Then roll out the pastry crust, place the roast in the centre and cover the roast with the crust, pinching the edges together. Place on a rack in a roaster and cook in a 350° oven. About 15 minutes before removing the roast from the oven, brush the crust with beaten egg yolks to give it a golden colour.

Serves 4.

# Melancholia

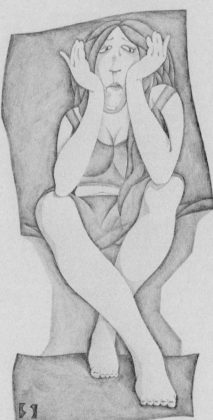

Melancholia refers to a chronic state of mild depression. Nothing seems quite right and every silver lining has a dark cloud. The melancholic person tends to be religious and to inter-personally pull rejection from others; he might, thus, join the Salvation Army and then get a Dear John letter. To live in melancholy is painful, but the Germans (who have a penchant for this solemn, gloomy disorder and who have almost perfected it) have also concocted this vegetable dish to go along with it. It is made from red cabbage which the Germans call, for some oppositional reason, blue.

## Blue Cabbage

1 medium head of red cabbage
1 tbsp. butter
1 chopped onion
2 apples, peeled, chopped and cored
2 tbsp. brown sugar
2 tbsp. vinegar

Put 2 to 3 cups of water in a sauce-pan and add the butter and cut-up cabbage. Add the onion, apples, and brown sugar and cook for about 45 minutes. Add the vinegar just before serving.

This is very tasty served with breaded pork chops and corn muffins.

# Multiple Personality

Probably the most dramatic and well-publicized neurotic syndrome is the multiple personality. In this condition, there is a disturbance of consciousness in which different aspects of the personality split off and emerge at different times as a total or dominant personality. One personality may be quite unaware of the existence of other personalities, which appear to possess radically different traits. This condition is exceedingly rare (if it exists at all in true form) but it has been the subject of many novels, movies, and paintings. In its mildest form, the dissociating process is reflected in the propensity of many of us to reject certain "unacceptable" aspects of ourselves. The "I'm not myself when I'm drunk," or "that just couldn't have been me that pinched the boss's wife" defence is a common attempt to consciously differentiate one part of a personality from another.

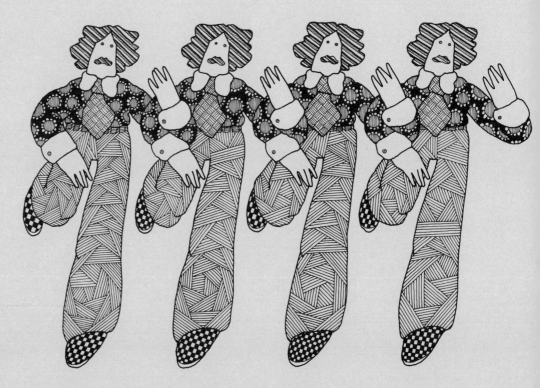

## Sauerbraten mit Yorkshire Pudding

4 lbs. top round of beef
2 onions, sliced
3 cloves
¾ cup of dry red wine
2 peppercorns, crushed
½ cup wine vinegar
2 large carrots, sliced
2 stalks celery, chopped
1 bay leaf
6 tbsp. butter
5 tbsp. flour
1 tbsp. sugar
salt and pepper
4 allspice berries

Season the beef with salt and pepper and place it in an earthenware, glass, or enamel bowl. Combine the onions, cloves, celery, carrots, allspice berries, wine vinegar, peppercorns, and bay leaf in a saucepan. Bring to boil and then pour it over the meat. The bowl is then put in the refrigerator for 2 days, covered and left to marinate. Turn it twice a day.

When ready to cook it, remove the meat and sear it quickly in butter on both sides until it is well-browned. Then pour the marinade back over it and bring to a boil, then turn it down and let simmer, covered, slowly for about 3 hours. Remove bay leaf, cloves, and peppercorns before serving by straining the broth.

Make a sauce by combining the melted 5 tbsp. butter with the flour and sugar until it is thoroughly blended and getting dark in colour. Mix a cup of the liquid from the roast with it until it is a smooth sauce, then add it to the simmering meat. Continue cooking about 30 minutes in a covered pot.

Serve this traditional German dish with Yorkshire Pudding.

2 eggs
1 cup flour
meat drippings (approx. ¼ cup)
1 cup milk
salt

In a large bowl combine the flour and salt. Break in the eggs and add 1 cup of milk, stirring slowly. Add, by degrees, the remainder of the milk until it is a rich, smooth batter. Beat it well, let it stand for 60 minutes, then beat it again for a few minutes. Heat a dish containing the meat drippings in the oven, pour the batter into it, and cook for 25 minutes at a medium heat.

Serves 4-6.

# Narcolepsy

Narcolepsy is a rare condition that begins in young adulthood. It is manifested by the sudden, irresistible impulse to sleep while standing or sitting. Sleep periods may last for hours or minutes. Early diagnosis can be especially helpful for aspiring cellists and airline pilots. Here is a recipe you might pass on to a narcoleptic (when the *zzzzz* sound stops) as it allows for a safe snooze.

## Cabbage Rolls and Rest

1 large cabbage
1 lb. ground chuck
1 onion (chopped fine)
1 large can of tomato sauce
1 cup of rice
½ tsp. cinnamon (ground)
dash of ginger
salt and pepper
1 cup water or beef broth

Parboil the cabbage quickly and set out to cool. In a large bowl, mix the raw ground beef, the onion, and rice. Remove the cabbage leaves and in each leaf place some of the meat and rice mixture. Roll up the stuffed leaves and arrange them in layers in a deep casserole dish.

Mix together the tomato sauce, water or broth, cinnamon, ginger, and salt and pepper. Pour over the cabbage rolls. Cover the casserole and place in a moderate oven or simmer slowly on a burner for 40 to 60 minutes.

(There is usually cabbage left over after the rolls are made. You can make a nice cabbage soup out of the leftovers.)

Serves 4.

# Nymphomania

Nymphomania is the urge to seek out repeated and various sexual encounters because the experiences are not fully satisfying.

## Chicken Chow Mein (Won Ton Hussy)

1 scallion, sliced
¼ lb. chicken, sliced thin
   (pork may be substituted)
1 can bamboo shoots
2 stalks celery, sliced thin
4 leaves of Chinese cabbage,
   sliced thin
3 tbsp. cooking oil
1 lb. egg noodles
½ cup water
12 string beans, julienned
½ tsp. M.S.G.
1 clove garlic, minced
1 cup stock of chicken broth
1 tsp. soy sauce
6 mushrooms, sliced
1 tsp. salt
6 snowpeas
1 tbsp. cornstarch
½ tsp. pepper

Boil the egg noodles for 7 to 9 minutes, rinse in cold water. Drain and brush a little oil on the noodles.

Then heat 2 tbsp. oil in hot skillet and drop in noodles to brown evenly. Stir frequently to prevent sticking. Add a little water if noodles start to harden too quickly. Add garlic to 1 tbsp. oil, then when very hot, drop in chicken. After browning the chicken, mix in the vegetables, the stock, and cover it. Cook several minutes. Blend soy sauce, M.S.G., water, cornstarch, salt and pepper and pour into pan. Stir occasionally while sauce thickens, then pour over noodles. Take off heat and garnish with scallion slices.

## Egg Foo Jung

4 eggs
½ lb. mushrooms
1 can water chestnuts, small
1 onion (chopped)
salt and pepper
3 cups cooked meat or chicken
   (cubed)
½ cup bean sprouts
   (or drained can of bean sprouts)
1 stalk celery (chopped)

In a bowl, beat eggs lightly. Add all the ingredients. Ladle one fourth egg mixture into frying plan and butter until golden on bottom. Turn carefully and cook the other side. Repeat until all the mixture is used.

*Gravy*

1 tbsp. cornstarch
1 tsp. soy sauce
¼ tsp. sugar
1½ cups chicken stock
1 tsp. salt, pepper

The gravy is made by blending cornstarch with the stock, soy sauce, salt, pepper, and sugar. Cook over a medium heat, stirring all the time. Just as it comes to a boil, turn it off and pour over the Foo Jung.

A nice addition to this is deep-fried prawns served with a Chinese mustard sauce and sesame seeds.

# Obsessive Compulsive Personality

The obsessive-compulsive tends to be a fastidious, rigid, extra-neat person who goes over and over things in his or her mind before taking action. Everything must be orderly, clean and as precise as possible. Obsessive-compulsive people do not usually enjoy dishes such as barbecued spareribs or that Hawaiian favourite, poi. So, if you only feel comfortable with an apron on your back as well as on your front, and you actually expect your guests at 8:00 when you tell them 8:00, this is the recipe for you. You may wish to begin obsessing about the ingredients as you're brushing your teeth, then around mid-afternoon carefully and compulsively start to follow the following recipe. Exactly. You'll want to wash your hands and face, of course, first.

**Perfectly Square Ravioli**

*Pasta*

2 eggs (not too large, on the other hand, not too small)
3 cups flour (the cup may be tin or plastic as long as it is a measuring cup)
¼ tsp. salt (to achieve the desired exactitude, scrape a knife blade across the edge of the ¼ tsp. which will remove any excess grains of salt. Catch the excess grains on a small piece of waxed paper, as they can be used again later in the recipe.)
2 tbsp. butter (perhaps your guests won't notice if you substitute margarine here, but you will know)
1 cup warm water (sort of lukewarm, just approaching tepid)

Sift the flour and salt together and place mixture on a breadboard. Drop the eggs in the exact centre, add the butter, and mix. Gradually add water until you have a rather stiff dough.

Knead until smooth, then cover and let stand for about 10 minutes. Cut the dough in half, then roll it out onto a lightly floured board until it is very thin. You can take a break here, to wash your hands again.

*Filling*

1 cup chopped spinach, cooked (the size of the spinach chops may be variable)
1 cup minced, cooked chicken (minced means smaller than "chopped", and larger than "ground")
½ cup bread crumbs
⅓ cup Parmesan cheese
2 eggs
2 tsp. chopped parsley
½ clove garlic, chopped
salt and pepper to taste (presumably yours)

Beat eggs lightly. Blend together all other ingredients. Gradually add

enough beaten egg to hold firmly together. Drop tsps. full of filling about 2 inches apart on one sheet of dough until filling is used up. Then cover this with another sheet of thinly rolled dough. With tips of fingers firmly press around each mound of filling to form a small puffed-up square. Each little square is full of filling and can then be cut apart from one another with a serrated edge pastry cutter.* Fill a large pot with absolutely 4 quarts of water and salt and bring to a boil. When water is boiling vigorously, cook ravioli for about 10 minutes (until the dough is tender). Remove them with a perforated spoon and top with a tomato sauce and Parmesan cheese.

Delicious as a main course with a salad composed of romaine lettuce, red chopped onions, fried bacon bits, and covered with an oil and vinegar dressing.

*If you have a T-square, you may wish to check your corners.

# Paranoia

Paranoia is a pathological state of mistrust and suspicion. The most severe stages are marked by delusions of persecution and bizarre thinking patterns. Many of us have some degree of paranoid ideas, and are capable of concluding that the Saint Bernard across the street has been diabolically trained to prefer our front yard, for instance. It isn't always easy to distinguish what is paranoid from what isn't, as "reality" is often elusive and complex. Perhaps the fifth Mrs. Bluebeard tried to tell her doctor that hubby was a bit odd. If you have a tinge of paranoia and don't want to be plotted against or talked about by your dinner guests, the following dish allows you to remain in the room with them at all times during the meal. It also provides you with a weapon should you suddenly need to defend yourself against a hostile Martian disguised as your brother-in-law.

**Paranoid Hot Pot**

a fondue pot
peanut oil
strips of lean beef
strips of white meat chicken
flowers of raw cauliflower

Heat the oil and dip in the strips of beef or other basic ingredients on individual fondue forks. Cook to taste, and dip in the following sauces.

*Pepper Sauce*

1 medium onion (minced)
2 tbsp. butter
½ green pepper (minced)
1 tsp. oregano
1 tsp. sweet basil
½ bottle chili sauce
dash of dry mustard
cup of cream or sour cream

Sauté the onion and green pepper in the butter until soft. Sprinkle with oregano and basil and add ½ bottle tomato chili sauce. Season with salt and pepper and dry mustard. Simmer for about 10 minutes and add cream or sour cream.

*Dill Sauce*

1 tbsp. butter
1 tbsp. flour
½ cup milk
½ cup white wine
2 tsp. dill weed

Blend the flour in the melted butter. Turn down the heat and slowly add the milk until blended. Add the wine and cook slowly until sauce is thickened and smooth. Add dill and salt and pepper.

*Horseradish Sauce*

1 cup sour cream
bottled horseradish (to taste)
chives

Blend sour cream, chives, horseradish and salt and pepper.

Serve with mixed greens with French dressing and hot biscuits.

# Perseveration

Perseveration is an abnormally persistent repetition or continuance of an idea. The initial idea or action may be appropriate but becomes pathological with its repeated execution. You should never telephone a perseverator long distance, unless all you want to hear is "Hello." But, if you are the perseverator, the following recipe will give you a little something to do in the kitchen, again, and again, and again.

## Enchilladas Encore

1 pkg. tortillas
1 large can tomato sauce
½ tsp. hot sauce
1 large onion (chopped or diced)
1 lb. cheddar cheese (diced)
1 lb. ground round
½ can water
1 pkg. prepared enchillada seasoning

Place a tortilla on a rack in a roaster or casserole. Sprinkle some cooked ground round on the tortilla, some tomato sauce thinned with ½ can of water into which the hot sauce and enchillada seasoning has been mixed, some chopped onions, and cheese. Put another tortilla on top and repeat. Keep up this happy repetition until you have run out of ingredients. Bake in a moderate oven for 30 minutes.

This is excellent served with shredded crisp lettuce and oil and vinegar. A side of re-fried beans (there are good canned ones available) complete this Mexican perseveration.

Serves 4.

# Polymorphous Perverse

This is a term which was coined by Freud and which is somewhat convoluted in meaning and connotation. "Poly" means many and "morphous" means kind (as in "morphous old lady"); "perverse" means "twisted." Translation from German, and particularly from Freudian German, is never easy nor quick, and is sometimes quite pointless. Thus, with the above phrase we might have a translation reading "many twisted old ladies" or perhaps "many kinds of twists" or even the more sonorous "numerous convoluted kinds." In all of these possibilities we may have the analytic roots of the modern dance.

However, the generally accepted version of Freud's term refers to the potential to be sexually attracted to any person, place, or thing; any object, subject, or predicate. Dr. Freud maintained that we are all born with this potential and that it is our society and our superego which limits and determines our sexual choices. He saw us all as potentially attracted to anything that moves; a blade of grass may be a passionflower to some.

We will offer a variety of dessert dishes here which could provide you and any polymorphous friends you might have with an orgy of sensate pleasures. All the recipes given have a certain élan which could easily stimulate those who are close to their own polymorphous needs.

### Strawberries Jubilee

Bring to a boil ½ cup of water, ⅓ of a cup of sugar, 2 teaspoons of cornstarch. Add about 1 pint of strawberries and bring them back to the boil, stirring gently to glaze the berries. Heat 2 oz. of kirsch and set it alight. Pour the strawberries over ice cream and the flaming kirsch over the strawberries. Serve immediately. (In order to add the right note of orgy, the last operations should be carried out with the entire dinner group assembled.)

## Chocolate Pie

Bake your own favourite pie crust or use a frozen or prepared pie crust. If you use the prepared ones cook them ahead of time and then add to them the following filling.

1 6-oz. package of semi-sweet
    chocolate
2 egg yolks
½ cup of sour cream
2 egg whites
⅓ cup of honey

Melt the chocolate and add the egg yolks over a low heat. Remove the mixture from the heat and add the sour cream. Beat the egg whites until they are stiff and add the honey while you are beating the whites. Then add the beaten whites to the chocolate and pour it into the crust and chill before serving.

## Banana Trifle

bananas (1 per person)
1 cup apricot jam
1½ jiggers brandy or rum
½ pint whipped cream

Mix the brandy or rum with the apricot jam a little ahead of serving so that the flavours blend. Just before serving, whip the cream, split the bananas lengthwise and spread the apricot jam over them. Top with the whipped cream and serve immediately.

## Coffee Bavarian Cream

2 envelopes of unflavoured gelatin
½ cup cold water
1 cup hot water
1 (15 oz.) can sweetened
    condensed milk
2 cups extra-strong coffee beverage
1 cup heavy cream
sweetened sliced fresh peaches
½ oz. brandy

In a large bowl mix the gelatin with the cold water. Add the hot water and stir until the gelatin is thoroughly dissolved. Add the condensed milk and the coffee and stir it well until it is blended.

Chill this until the mixture begins to thicken. Whip the cream and fold it into the gelatin mixture. Pour it into a 6-cup mould which has been chilled. Put it in the refrigerator and when it has set, unmould it.
Serve with the peach slices which have been well-mixed with the brandy, and with additional whipped cream if you prefer a richer and more sensuous finale.

# Psychoanalysis

Psychoanalysis is one form of psychotherapy originally conceived by Freud which involves a specific kind of relationship between patient and analyst. The analyst systematically attempts to uncover the roots of the patient's current personality problems by exploring the deeper layers of the patient's mind. He strives to pull away defences in order to explore the developmental core of the personality. The goal is to then bring about an alteration in the individual's personality structure by undoing the effects of the past, and subsequently reorganizing the unfavourable patterns that had been established in early childhood. It's as if the patient were an artichoke and the analyst a gourmet, carefully uncovering each leafy layer, in search of the heart of the matter. It is an expensive process which usually takes many years to complete because of its complexity. (Did you ever try to rebuild an artichoke?)

## Stuffed Artichokes

The artichoke is often a sadly neglected vegetable that can be delicious served hot or cold. The following recipe is for cold artichokes which are cooked, chilled, and stuffed.

4 *large* firm artichokes
1 cup ground ham or liver sausage
½ tsp. dry mustard
¼ tsp. turmeric
¾ cup mayonnaise
1 clove garlic, minced
¼ cup minced onion
salt and pepper

Cook the artichokes in rapidly boiling water for 40 to 60 minutes. Test to see if they are done by pulling gently on an outside leaf. If it comes off easily, the artichoke is cooked. When done, set out to cool.

In a bowl, mix the ground ham or liver sausage. Add the mayonnaise, minced onion, garlic, mustard, turmeric, salt and pepper. Make a smooth paste of this mixture. Do not hesitate to use more mayonnaise if it is needed to make the mixture thinner for easy dipping.

Take the cool artichoke and spread apart the leaves where they close together at the top. You can reach down to the bottom then and clean out the feathery thistle section which protects the heart of the plant. When this is scooped out, spoon in the ham mixture and set in the refrigerator to chill.

When eating the artichoke, the tender ends of the leaves are dipped into the ham mixture.

1 per person.

# Pyromania

Pyromania refers to compulsive fire-setting, and the pyromaniacal individual experiences an element of sexual gratification from this activity. People with these tendencies enjoy chefing the company "weinie-roast" and can be observed gleefully flinging the starter fluid hither and yon as they dance about. The true pyromaniac's picnic, however, was typified in the good old-fashioned witch-hunts. Since these Salem cook-outs are becoming obsolete, pyromania is outdated and often dangerous. Burning, at its best, belongs in the kitchen, and can be beautifully expressed in this simple dessert.

## Bananas Flambé

4 bananas
4 tbsp. butter
4 tbsp. brown sugar
2 tsp. lemon juice
2 to 3 oz. rum or cognac
1 tsp. lemon rind, grated

Peel the bananas and cut them lengthwise. Put them in a shallow baking dish that has been greased lightly. Mix the butter (melted), the lemon juice, and the brown sugar together and pour over the bananas. Bake in a medium oven for about 10 minutes.

When you remove them from the oven, serve at the table. Pour 2 to 3 oz. of heated rum or cognac over the bananas and ignite them.

# Rorschach Inkblot Test

The Rorschach inkblot test was designed by a Swiss psychiatrist whose name was Hermann Inkblot. He discovered that if you take a piece of paper and dab a rorschach on it the results are a symmetrical blot which seems to stimulate the imaginations of people the way cloud formations produce visual fantasies on lazy hillside afternoons. The inkblot test is used to delve into the unconscious fantasies of the inkblot gazer by promoting his unique, individualized projections onto the unstructured stimulus. (A large glob of melting chocolate will produce some of the same phenomena and some advantages in that you can eat your fantasy afterward.)

There are many ways to score and to evaluate projective instruments such as the inkblot test. It is, in fact, a complex diagnostic tool. The main theory holds that individual personality traits can be seen through the projected creations of the viewer. For example, people who see only people in the ink blot forms are different from people who see only tubas — who are different again from people who see only inkblots.

Almost any dish with a sauce can serve as a projective technique if you care to look closely. Try projecting onto this unstructured stimulus.

## Ham and Beef Rouladen

2 cups sliced mushrooms
½ cup green onions (chopped)
2 tbsp. butter or margarine
6 thin slices cooked beef or
  6 minute steaks
6 thin slices cooked ham
salt and pepper
1 cup beef broth
¼ cup dry sherry or Madeira
1 tbsp. flour
1 clove garlic (crushed)
½ tsp. thyme

Sauté the sliced mushrooms and the chopped green onions in 1 tbsp. butter or margarine for about 5 minutes. Place the slices of cooked beef or the thin steaks and the slices of ham together and put about 3 tbsp. of the mushroom filling in the centre of each ham and beef slice. Roll up the slices. Place them in a baking dish.

Combine the beef broth and the sherry or Madeira, the crushed garlic, the thyme and salt and pepper. In a saucepan melt 1 tbsp. of butter or margarine and blend in the flour. When they are well blended, add the wine and broth juices and bring to a boil, then remove from the heat. Pour the sauce over the meat rolls and cover the dish. Bake for 20 minutes at 350°.

Serve this simple, tasty meat entrée with potato salad, French bread, and fresh sliced tomatoes sprinkled with oil and vinegar.

# Sadism

Sadism is a type of erotic satisfaction derived from inflicting pain. A sadist enjoys hurting others. He is the type of person, for instance, who would hold the Weight Watchers' Convention in a bakery, or serve corn-on-the-cob to the Senior Citizens' Committee. With such morbid enthusiasm for cruelties, sadists commonly have difficulty with their public relations. They often offend others. So, if you wish to avoid possibly unpleasant reprisals, I would recommend that you channel your sadistic impulses into culinary activities. These tasty chicken recipes provide excellent opportunities to revel in hostile aggression, and the results are more than acceptable.

First of all, tear the skin off a cut-up fryer. Then insert a small sharp knife into the chicken and carefully cut the flesh away from the bones. (Save the bones and the skin for soup, etc.) A boned chicken affords easier eating. So even if you are not sadistic, the boning process is well worth the effort.

After you've torn the beast apart, here are two quick and excellent ways to dispose of the remains.

## Chicken à la Sade

cut up and boned breast and thigh
    parts of 2 chickens
¼ cup chopped mushrooms
4 tbsp. butter
2 tsp. cornstarch
¼ cup light cream
¾ cup chopped Swiss cheese
1 tbsp. chopped pimento
1 tbsp. chopped parsley
dash of cayenne
3 tbsp. flour
1 egg, beaten
fine bread crumbs
salt and pepper

Sauté the chopped mushrooms in 2 tbsp. butter. Blend in the cornstarch, add the cream and cook until very thick. Add the Swiss cheese and the seasonings, including the pimento. Cook until the cheese melts and then blend in the parsley. Set it aside and chill it thoroughly. After it is chilled, stuff the chicken with the mixture. Dust the breast with flour, then dip in the beaten egg and then in the bread crumbs. Sauté in 2 tbsp. butter until golden brown.

Then place the stuffed chicken parts in a low baking dish and finish the cooking in a moderate (350°) oven for about 20 minutes.

This is a very tasty way to serve chicken and should be accompanied by a fairly plain vegetable and potato or rice dish.

### Chicken Meany

4 whole cut-up fryer breasts
1 can tomato sauce, large
1 pkg. mozzarella cheese
salt and pepper
1 cup fine bread crumbs
1 egg
dash of oregano
3 tbsp. butter

After you bone the chicken, dip the parts in one beaten egg and then in the fine bread crumbs. Heat butter to foaming and quickly fry the chicken parts on both sides. When they are brown, quickly remove them to a shallow casserole, pour over the tomato sauce, salt and pepper, and add slices of mozzarella. Using freshly crumbled or prepared oregano, sprinkle the chicken lightly with the seasoning and place it in a moderate (350°) oven for about 30 minutes. The cheese will melt and bubble and the chicken will remain crisp beneath the cheese sauce.

This is particularly nice served with hot rolls, fresh salad vegetables, and flat noodles for the sauce.

Serves 4.

# Sibling Rivalry

If you are an only child, you have never experienced the joy of hating someone simply because you shared a mother – siblings aren't small sibs. A sibling is any brother or sister of any size, at any time and if you have a sib, you have a sibling rivalry. There's only room on the lap for one at a time and whoever is left off is the rivalrous sib. The other one is known technically as a spoiled brat.

This problem is harder to work out if you are an only child because there is no one else to blame except mother (see guilt). Sometimes parents try to compensate for a lack of siblings by comparing you unfavourably to the child next door who always seems to play the piano gratefully and well and who never fails to take out the garbage well before the truck arrives. But if you are lucky enough to have a sibling to hate, you might steal her

favourite recipe and do it better or cook this and invite her (and your mother) over and then pretend you whipped it up at the last minute. The nice thing about this dish is that you can casually refer to it as "just some leftovers."

## Crêpes Nicole

*Crêpes\**

for 12 crêpes
1 cup cold water
1 cup cold milk
4 eggs
½ tsp. salt
1 cup sifted flour
4 tbsp. melted butter

*Sauce Béchamel*

2 tbsp. butter
2 tbsp. flour
⅔ cup milk
½ cup chicken stock or broth
salt and pepper

86

*Filling*

2 cups cooked chicken
1 tbsp. butter
1 tbsp. paprika
½ cup chopped cooked mushrooms
cream or milk
1 egg yolk
grated cheese

*If you're not a purist you can make a thin crêpe batter using 1 cup of prepared pancake mix, mixed very thin with a tbsp. of rum or brandy added.

*Crêpes:* This batter is made with the electric blender because it is very quick and makes a smooth blend. Pour the liquids, eggs, and salt into the blender. Cover it and turn on top speed for 1 minute. Cover and refrigerate for at least 2 hours. About 15 minutes before you are to serve take the batter mix and make thin pancakes about six inches in diameter.

These are best made in a small crêpe pan but a well-balanced, evenly heated frying pan will do as well. Keep the crêpes thin and cook them quickly. They can be kept out after making them as the entire dish will be popped into the oven to heat before serving. Now prepare the filling and the sauce.

*Sauce:* Blend together the melted butter and the flour in a saucepan over a low heat. Slowly add the milk and then the chicken broth, stirring it until it becomes a smooth, rich sauce. Season with salt and pepper.

*Filling:* Cube the cooked chicken and toss the cubes in hot butter, well-seasoned with paprika. Add to the chicken a few chopped cooked mushrooms and just enough cream to moisten the mixture. Keep this hot.

Place a little of the chicken mixture on each pancake and roll them up and arrange them on an ovenproof dish.

To the Béchamel sauce add the egg yolk and a bit of cream and pour it over the crêpes. Sprinkle them with grated cheese and run them under the broiler until they are bubbly.

Garnish with cold asparagus spears and serve with hot rolls. These crêpes are elegant and different.

Serves 3-4.

# Satyriasis or Don Juanism

Satyriasis is the masculine equivalent of nymphomania – the "conquest to conquest" compulsion. This amalgam of behaviours is found in many walks of life: the movie director and the quarterback have it easy; it's more difficult for a balding plumber. (A few well known analysts suffer from this syndrome and are eminently successful as they charge $50.00 an hour as well.) In fantasy life most men are prone to the prone and they may well identify with this hot skewer playboy menu. With the proper grill, the dinner can be left to broil while Don Juan attends to the guest or guests. Overnight marinating adds a lecherous note.

## Shashlik

1 lb. lamb meat, cubed
tiny whole tomatoes
small whole onions, parboiled
back (Canadian) bacon
juice of 2 lemons
1 tbsp. parsley
1 tbsp. dill weed
2 garlic cloves
salt and pepper
½ cup water

Place the cubed lamb in a bowl or earthenware pot. Season it with salt and pepper, parsley, chopped garlic cloves, and dill weed to suit your taste. Mix the lemon juice with ½ cup of water and marinate overnight.

When ready to cook the lamb, take the pieces out, dry them, and string them on skewers. Alternate the cubes of meat with tiny parboiled onions, cherry tomatoes, and pieces of bacon. Or you can string the vegetables on separate skewers as they may cook more quickly than the meats.

This is excellent served with wild rice and slices of raw apples and oranges with a sour cream dressing. This dressing is made simply by adding 1 teaspoon of lemon juice to ½ cup of sour cream.

Serves 4.

# Somnambulism

When a person executes a relatively complicated task while in some stage of sleep, he is a somnambulist. This form of "sleepwalking" occurs during certain phases of sleep in which brain wave activity indicates there is no dreaming. The condition may surprise others in the house and in the neighbourhood, but it is not to be considered indicative of a serious psychological disturbance.

Many a small-town somnambulist has achieved notoriety when he wandered on stage during the Little Theatre's first act of *Hamlet.** If you know a somnambulist who would like to stay up a little longer after dinner and before the theatre, you might suggest this smooth, coffee liqueur.

**Coffee Liqueur**

¾ cup hot water
⅓ cup instant coffee powder
2 cups sugar
2 cups vodka
1 tsp. vanilla

In a saucepan, slowly heat the hot water, instant coffee, and sugar until the sugar dissolves. Add the vodka and vanilla and blend thoroughly. Store in a dark container in a cool place.

*For seasonal variation, they often draped a chain around him and did Dicken's *A Christmas Carol*.

# Tension Headache

Persons prone to these types of headaches are generally driving, perfectionistic individuals who may also be subject to the more severe migraine attacks. Tension headaches involve pain in the back of the head as well as the front and also in the shoulders and neck region. The pain is from prolonged contracture of cervical muscles. This tightening can be a somatic component of chronic anxiety as well as of conflictual tension.

If, one evening, you find that your usually efficient but tempermental hostess has just been undone by one of those "terrible headaches" and has left her planned meatloaf undone in the kitchen, step in confidently. Place her on a rectangular, ungreased couch and cover her head with a wet dish towel. She will rise when ready. Then dash to the kitchen and quickly prepare this instant gourmet dish for yourself and the other ravenous guests.

**Steak Tartare**

1 lb. steak, finely ground
2½ tsp. dry mustard
1 onion, small
1½ tsp. salt
1 clove garlic
several dashes of Worcestershire
    sauce
1 cup parsley, chopped
ground black pepper (optional)

Grate the onion and garlic. Mix all ingredients in a bowl and work into a smooth patty. Serve on platter decoratively surrounded with slices of rye bread.

A simple lettuce salad with tomato wedges, thinly sliced mushrooms and Bermuda onions, topped with lemon juice makes a nice accompaniment.

Serves 2-3.

# Voyeurism

Voyeurism means deriving sexual enjoyment from peeking or peering at others who are in some state of undress. It is the furtive aspect of the viewing that provides the pleasure . . . the kick is in the peep. Since peeping Toms and Thomasinas are bound to lower the shades and raise the ire of neighbours, it's best to keep this little quirk at home. So if voyeurism is your peccadillo, it is probably worth your while to invest in an oven with a window in the door. You may wish to drape a tea towel over the window for an added spicy effect, and peek away in your own kitchen at:

## Undressed Breast of Chicken

2 tbsp. butter
1 garlic clove
6 slices of cheese (cheddar or Swiss)
6 halves of chicken breast (boned)
6 ham slices
6 slices of bacon

*Sauce*

1 medium onion (chopped)
1 tsp. paprika
salt and pepper
2 tbsp. butter
2 tbsp. flour
1 cup chicken broth or stock
2 tbsp. chives or green onion

Bone the halved chicken breasts and place them between two pieces of waxed paper. With a knife handle or mallet, flatten the breasts. Then rub fresh minced garlic on the inside of each breast and add a slice of cooked ham and a slice of cheese. Roll up each breast and wrap around each a slice of bacon.

Cook in a frying pan, over medium heat, in butter, turning frequently to insure uniform cooking.

*Sauce*

Melt 2 tbsp. butter in saucepan, add the chopped onions and sauté until wilted. Add the flour and blend thoroughly. Then add the paprika and chives and slowly pour in the chicken stock, stirring the whole time until the sauce is smooth and fairly thick.

The chicken breasts and sauce are lovely served with asparagus with fresh lemon juice and crusty French rolls.

Serves 3-4.

# Xenophobia

Xenophobia is the heightened fear of foreigners or strangers. Would you crouch in the corner with a 5 lb. tranquillizer if you were suddenly thrust into the U.N.? Do you become slightly liver-kneed if a new mailman comes on your route? Does the sight of your father-in-law coming from a Shriners' convention give you the chills? You've got Xenophobia.

Handle it by progressively desensitizing yourself to all things foreign. Start with something tasty such as Chiou Tzu.

## Chiou Tzu

½ lb. raw pork
¼ lb. raw shrimp, shelled and
   deveined
½ cup oil
⅓ cup onions, finely chopped
1 tsp. ginger root, finely chopped
3 tbsp. soy sauce
½ tsp. sugar
1 tsp. salt
2 cups flour
1 egg
1 cup cold water

Grind the pork and the shrimp. Heat 2 tbsp. oil in a skillet; sauté the chopped onions and the ginger for about 3 minutes. Add the pork mixture to the skillet and sauté for another 5 minutes. Stir this frequently and then blend in the soy sauce, sugar, and salt and set it aside to cool.

Sift the flour into a bowl and make a well in the centre of the flour. Put the eggs and ½ cup water into the centre of the flour and work it in. Knead it until it is a smooth and elastic paste. Cover it with a bowl and let it sit for about 20 minutes. Then roll it out on waxed paper and cut it into 3 inch circles.

Put two teaspoons of the filling on each of the circles and fold them over, being sure to seal the edges well.

Heat the remaining oil in a skillet and arrange the dumplings in the oil in rows. Fry until the bottom of each is slightly browned. Add ½ cup of water. Cover and cook for 10 minutes over a low heat.

Serve these very tasty Chinese delicacies with hot mustard, duk sauce, and a small bowl of vinegar for dunking lightly.

Makes about 30 small dumplings.

# Zeitgarnik Effect

This phenomenon is named after its chief investigators, the Drs. Zeitgarnik. It is the tendency to remember tasks or events which are incomplete and to forget those which have been finished. After working for several years on this effect they completed their work – and promptly forgot it. Fortunately, they recorded their findings and left them to posterity.

**Complete German Potato Salad**

6 medium potatoes boiled in
   their jackets
1 tsp. sugar
½ cup of vinegar*
1 medium sliced onion
4 slices smoky, lean bacon (diced)
½ cup hot water
salt and pepper

Boil the potatoes in their jackets in salted water. While they boil, slice the onion into fine, thin slices. Marinate the onions in the vinegar, hot water, sugar, salt and pepper.

When the potatoes are done, drain them and let them stand a few minutes. Then, while they are still hot, peel them and slice them into ¼ -inch slices and add them to the onions in the marinade.

Fry the diced bacon until it is crisp. Add the bacon and the bacon fat to the potatoes and toss *lightly*. Do not toss them about too vigorously as the potatoes, when warm, tend to get mushy if shaken too enthusiastically. Serve while still warm.

This variation on potato salad is excellent with sausages or with pork dishes and it adds flavour and style to plain meat dishes.

*The amount and type of vinegar used depends on the cook and on how sharp you want the salad to be. Some vinegars are quite mild while others have a sharp bite and they should be tested before using.